LIFE IN BRAMPTON
WITH THE DANDY

LIFE IN BRAMPTON WITH THE DANDY

DAVID MOORAT

First published by
History Into Print, 56 Alcester Road,
Studley, Warwickshire B80 7LG in 2018
www.history-into-print.com

© David Moorat 2018

All rights reserved.

ISBN: 978-1-85858-351-8

The moral right of the author has been asserted.

A Cataloguing in Publication Record
for this title is available from the British Library.

Typeset in Haarlemmer MT Std.
Printed in Great Britain by
Bell & Bain Ltd.

CONTENTS

	Acknowledgements	6
1.	Introduction	7
2.	But Why The Term "Dandy"?	9
3.	So, When And Why Did This All Start?	11
4.	A Railway With Steam Locomotives On The Horizon For Brampton?	17
5.	A New Branch Line Begins To Take Shape	22
6.	But, Trouble Right From The Start	27
7.	Meetings, Protests, Petitions, Proposals, Counter Proposals... All Come To Nothing	33
8.	A New Dawn Breaks Over The Future For Brampton's Railway Facilities?	45
9.	The "New Dawn" Turns Into An "Early Sunset"	51
10.	Lady Rosalind Howard To The Rescue	56
11.	The New Dawn Has Finally Arrived	62
12.	Oh No, Not Again?	69

ACKNOWLEDGEMENTS

I am greatly indebted to many people who have been so helpful during the course of research for this publication: Staff at Cumbria Archive Office for their forbearance, cheerfulness and professionalism; Stephen White of The Lanes Library Carlisle, for access to the Jackson Collection, and to Denis Perriam, Carlisle historian for much guidance.

Most of the old photographs are reproduced with kind permission of Iain Parsons. I am grateful to Brampton artist Mr Stephen Warnes, BA GRA for providing the illustrations for the covers.

Last but by no means least, I am very grateful to my personal friends who have urged me on and given much support when my spirits were low.

Chapter 1

INTRODUCTION

In 1871 a scathing report appeared in the Carlisle Journal, severely criticising the travelling arrangements for those rail passengers wishing to get to Brampton.

> *"... in these days, when rapid locomotion is one of the chief requirements of the trader and of passengers, to be far removed from railways means nothing short of commercial death.*
>
> *Let us endeavour to realize the position of the place. Brampton as our readers are aware, lies nine miles due east of Carlisle, in the midst of a fertile agricultural district. The nearest railway station is at Milton, eleven or twelve miles from Carlisle, at which point the Newcastle Railway intersects the colliery line between Lord Carlisle's pits and Brampton. Here the passenger steps out upon an uncovered platform and enters a small Dandy Waggon – as it is locally termed – and in which first, second, and third class passengers are huddled together promiscuously – and is drawn by a horse for about three quarters of a mile, and then run down an incline without motive power for another stretch of about the same distance, until he is landed at the coal staith.*
>
> *The town of Brampton is still from half to three quarters of a mile distant, there are neither conveyances nor porters to be procured, and, as in bad weather the roads are ankle deep in mud, the luckless traveller is seldom well satisfied with himself for undertaking the expedition or with the railway company for deluding him into it. It should also be observed that although*

the company name Brampton on their time bills, they only in fact book to Milton, the service between Milton and the coal staith being charged extra; so that the passenger from Carlisle who wishes to reach this little town nine miles off, has to travel eleven or twelve miles by railway train, say a couple of miles more in a horsed wagon, for which he has to pay an extra fare and then to find himself landed from half to three quarters of a mile still distant from his destination."

Carlisle Journal, 7 November, 1871

What were the reasons for this unfortunate state of affairs for travellers, and why was the name of "Dandy" given to this apparently uncomfortable mode of travel?

This book sets out to trace the events, retells the incidents which took place and discusses the social and political pressures that brought about this unfortunate set of circumstances that left Brampton town without a convenient railway station.

Chapter 2

BUT WHY THE TERM "DANDY"?

In 1784, the term "Dandy" was regularly used in society:

"to describe something or someone that was remarkable; wonderful; superior; – something outrageously fashionable or eye-catching; something excellent in its class."

Oxford English Dictionary

None of these descriptions could remotely apply to the rather old fashioned, inconvenient, and uncomfortable method of travel that is described in our introduction from the Carlisle Journal of 1871.

The term is most certainly attributable to an early form of rail travel that did not involve steam locomotives but used horse power instead. In the early days of coal mining and quarry working, horses were used to haul wagons along a rail line. At the point where the rail line began to descend an incline, a brake was applied; the horse was unhitched and loaded onto a special cart at the rear. The brake would then be released and the wagons together with horse and cart would roll down the incline under the force of gravity, the driver applying the brake on approaching the destination!

George Stephenson (railway engineer 1781-1848) introduced the idea of a Dandy in 1828 which was simply a four-wheeled cart supplied with hay, for the horse to enjoy a period of rest with fresh food whilst allowing gravity to continue their onward journey.

An example of George Stephenson's "Dandy" cart.

Chapter 3

SO, WHEN AND WHY DID THIS ALL START?

Until the 1700s, agriculture and its supporting crafts were the main source of activity and livelihood in and around Brampton, but soon this was to change substantially with the discovery and exploitation of coal.

Particularly to the East of Brampton on lands owned by Lord Carlisle and the Naworth Estates, the winning of coal became a major industry. The mines were mainly drift mines – tunnels dug into hillsides. Horses were used to haul tubs or small wagons full of coal on wooden rails out of the tunnels to the surface.

Coal was then transferred into larger "Chaldron" wagons drawn by horses along lanes into Brampton where it was sold and used.

After a few years, the lanes had become deeply rutted, muddy and poorly maintained to such a degree that in 1790, Lord Carlisle's agent suggested abandoning the use of lanes and instead, extending the wooden rail system from

Chaldron wagons.

Horse power.

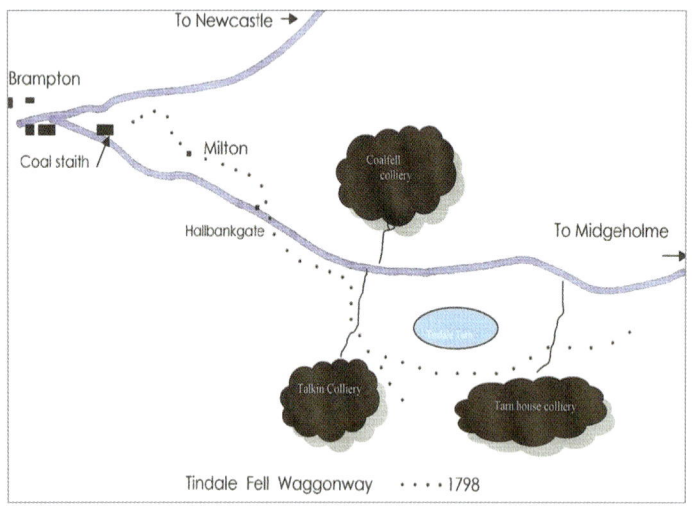

Naworth coal fields. DM archive.

the mine entrance, across the moor and fields via Hallbankgate and Milton to Brampton where a collection and distribution centre for the coal could be built.

By early 1799 the new wooden railed waggonway to Brampton was completed and was opened on the 15th April with a great celebration:

3. SO, WHEN AND WHY DID THIS ALL START?

> ❧ Laſt week a new rail-road (commonly called, in this neighbourhood, a *waggon-way*) was opened between the EARL of CARLISLE'S coal-works and the town of Brampton, in this county. An immenſe number of people aſſembled on the occaſion. The firſt waggon contained a band of muſic; ſeven others followed, loaden with coals.—A quantity of ale was given to the populace, at the market-croſs; and this new work, which promiſes great advantage to the neighbourhood, was hailed with every demonſtration of joy.

Carlisle Journal, 1799

The terminus of the waggonway was at the coal staithes, three quarters of a mile from the centre of Brampton.

The terminus. I. Parsons.

The terminus building still exists today. DM Archive.

From the coal staithes, the course of the waggonway ran parallel to today's Station Road in Brampton, behind houses further up that road, over fields to Cumcatch, crossing the current Newcastle railway line just north of the level crossing at Milton then on to Hallbankgate. On the Brampton Railway map below this is shown as "The old formation".

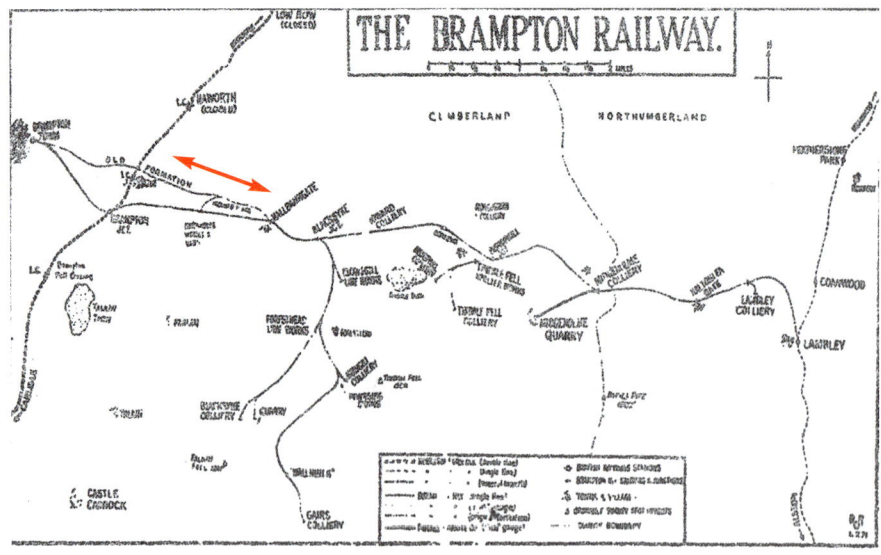

Route of the 1799 waggonway (The old formation). Brian Webb.

3. SO, WHEN AND WHY DID THIS ALL START?

The Greenwood map of 1823 shows the route of the waggonway with a curious sharp bend between Warren House and Cumcatch known locally as "Clarty turn":

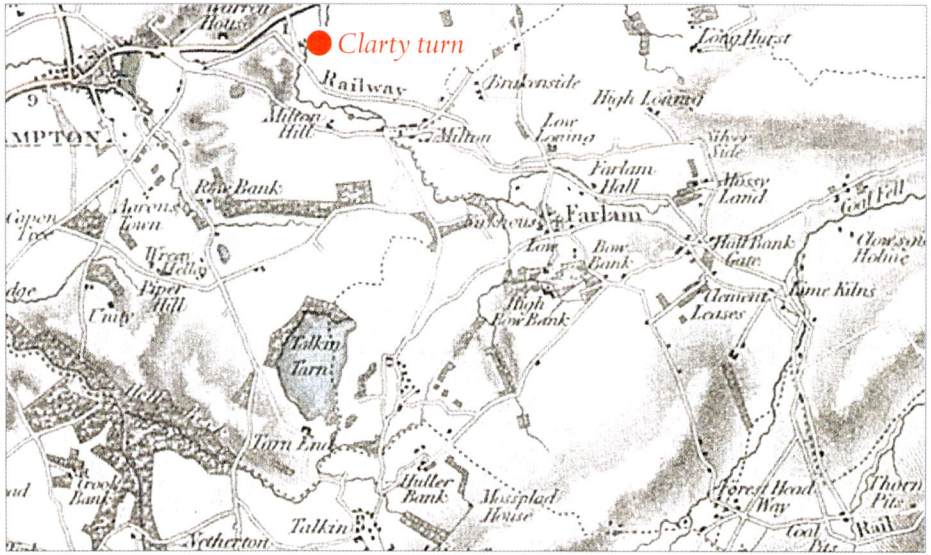

Greenwood map.

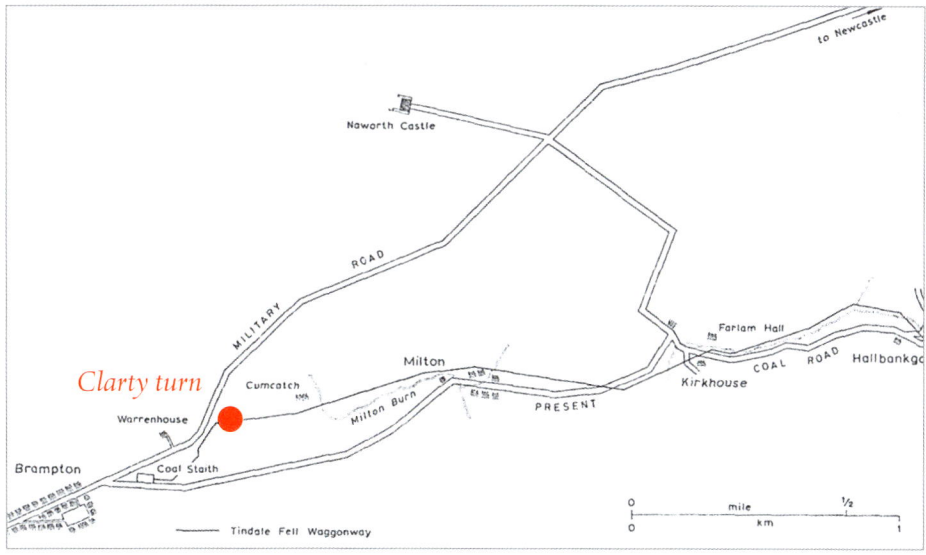

Clarty turn. Brian Webb.

15

The very first wagon of coal to arrive at the coal staithes was on 15th April 1799 hauled by a horse led by Mr Menzies, whose son later became the principal driver of the Dandy passenger carriage between Milton and Brampton. At the coal staithes a weighing and counting house was constructed – here the coal was transferred into sacks ready for sale and delivery.

Weighing house. Ian Parsons.

For the next twenty years this horse drawn system served the town of Brampton with coal and lime – **BUT NOT FOR PASSENGERS.**

Soon, exciting new developments were taking place up and down the country – the Industrial Revolution had arrived with the coming of:

Steam power.

Chapter 4

A RAILWAY WITH STEAM LOCOMOTIVES ON THE HORIZON FOR BRAMPTON?

Lord Carlisle, anxious to exploit to its maximum the coal reserves in and around the Naworth estates, gave instructions in 1825 to replace the horse drawn service and ageing wooden rail line with a railway for locomotives which should use the new standard gauge of 4 feet 8½ inches and use cast iron rails as recommended by the up and coming railway engineer George Stephenson. The first section from Hallbankgate to Midgeholme took three years to build.

James Thompson, a man of limitless energy and enterprise, had entered the service of Lord Carlisle in 1808. Ten years later, he took over the general agency of the coalmines and transport system. Being one of the earliest engineers to appreciate the value of steam power and the development of locomotive engines, he became a very close friend of George Stephenson. Thompson took over the leasehold of the Naworth collieries and established a depot at Kirkhouse to house sawmills, wagon shops, gas works, coke ovens, a foundry and engineering shops capable of building locomotives. Lord Carlisle clearly remained the owner of the estate land but a new company – James Thompson and Sons – was formed to manage the lease, which included the collieries, the workforce, the railway line and workshops.

Meanwhile, rail companies up and down the country had begun investing in building railways and in the north of England the Newcastle and Carlisle

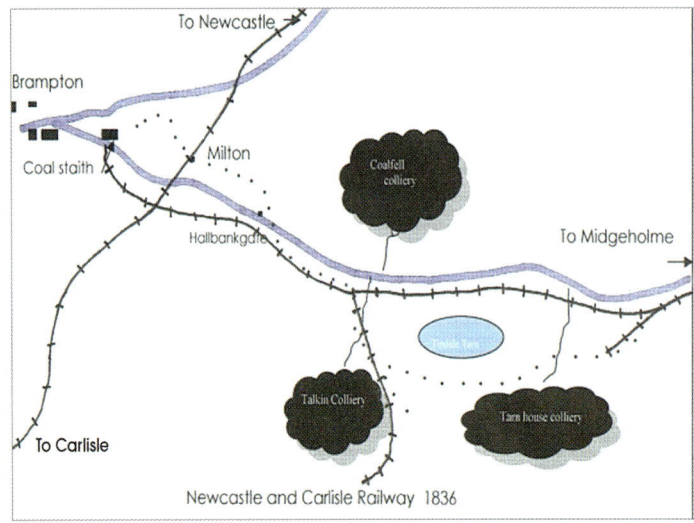

Intersection Newcastle to Carlisle Railway with Naworth coal lines. DM archive.

The cost of a single ticket from Milton to Carlisle was one shilling.

Milton Station (later renamed Brampton Junction).

Railway Company began negotiations to join the two towns of Newcastle and Carlisle by rail.

James Thompson urged Lord Carlisle to press for the Newcastle and Carlisle Railway to build their line to the **south** of Brampton rather than to the north. Lord Carlisle, immediately recognising the opportunity that such a rail line could bring to his coal business by opening up markets in Carlisle and eastwards to Newcastle, agreed and used much personal influence to encourage the directors of the railway company to arrange for the new rail line to intersect with his coal rail lines near Milton.

In 1836 the Newcastle to Carlisle line was duly completed, with a station at Milton for handling both passengers and freight.

Under the new arrangements, Lord Carlisle was now able to charge eight shillings and ten pence for a ton of coal in Carlisle, whilst in Brampton the same coal fetched only six shillings and eight pence. Whilst the modern rail system was being established between Carlisle and Newcastle, which was to give Lord Carlisle's coal works connections to the national network, a better link between Milton station and the town of Brampton became necessary.

Lord Carlisle's colliery agent James Thompson advised abandoning the now ageing wooden wagon way and, proposed the building of a new branch line directly to Brampton via Rowbank woods and Milton Hill, using the modern iron rail system designed by his friend George Stephenson.

Public opinion about the proposed route was divided. The lack of a station close to the centre of Brampton had become a major irritant to most of the townspeople. Many accused Lord Carlisle of using his influence to have the Newcastle to Carlisle line pass through his Milton coal works junction in order to take advantage of the increased trade opportunities rather than serving the needs of the travelling public abandoned in Brampton two miles away. Others, however, were fearful over the uncertainties of a changing world; afraid for themselves, their women and their cows!

Also, some shop owners felt that a rail station in the centre of Brampton would only encourage customers to travel elsewhere to buy their provisions with Brampton shops losing trade as a result.

Fear of "Iron Horses"

WHEN the Newcastle to Carlisle Railway was being built in the 1830's the people of Brampton refused to have anything to do with it, one reason being fear that the new "iron horses" would eventually do away with the need for live horses, which would conflict with their interests as an agricultural district. They also feared they would frighten their cows and their womenfolk!

TO THE EDITOR OF THE BRAMPTON HERALD.

Sir,—There has been a great deal of talk about a Railway coming into the town, many people think it will do the town good and increase its trade, and the consequence is, that everybody seems to want it. I know I am in the minority, but I dont see exactly how it is to be such a benefit: Look at other towns to which the railway has been extended, their trade is gone, and, my fear is, when we have got what we ask for, we shall find the same lot our own. People when they get into the train will go on to Carlisle, and other towns, instead of getting out at Brampton, and we shopkeepers here stand a great chance of being snuffed out by the enterprising traders of these places. But if it is not too late for us to think of the other side of the question, and, though I am but a small tradesman, I should not like to loose my chance of getting a living from customers who now prefer to visit my shop. **MEASURE FOR MEASURE**

Some felt that despite their pleas and efforts to petition the Newcastle and Carlisle Rail Company, the directors were unwilling to listen:

"The inhabitants of the town were not to blame for the Newcastle railway not passing through the town, for I myself, at that time a very young man, called upon almost every inhabitant of the town to ask them to sign a petition in favour of the line coming through the town, and I believe only three men called upon refused to sign it, but when I presented the petition to the directors, they gave me the cold shoulder."

L. Carrick. Coroner East Cumberland

Chapter 5

A NEW BRANCH LINE BEGINS TO TAKE SHAPE

Whereas the "old formation" track ran parallel to the Alston road, the new branch line was to cross the Alston road with a stone arch bridge in order to carry the line over the road towards Rowbank Woods and Milton station.

Post Card. DM Archive.

5. A NEW BRANCH LINE BEGINS TO TAKE SHAPE

Post Card. DM Archive.

During the construction of the new branch line into Brampton, many Irish navvies were employed to carry out the excavations. Temporary wooden huts were built close to the proposed rail line to provide accommodation for the navvies. The presence of scores of Irish labourers in Brampton certainly made an impact upon the town.

> *"An unexpected and noisy interruption to the divine service at St. Martin's Church, Sunday last was dealt with immediately by the churchwardens and Reverend Whitehead. During the sermon, shouting and brawling could be heard coming from the street outside. Bringing the service to an abrupt halt Reverend Whitehead together with church wardens sallied forth into the melee, to find a number of Irish labourers some stripped to the waist, fighting in the street, whilst others very much the worse for drink hurraaing and urging them on. The reverend announcing that he would not have such behaviour on the Lord's day, summoned the constable and gave instructions*

Milton Hill cutting.

Embankment, Rowbank Woods.

that the culprits be charged to appear in the magistrates court the following day. The unfortunate pugilists were not aware that the Reverend Whitehead is also our local magistrate."

Carlisle Journal, November, 1835

Using picks, spades, horses and carts, the navvies excavated thousands of tons of soil from Milton Hill to form a deep cutting – the spoil taken along the proposed route to Rowbank Woods to form an embankment; resulting in a more or less level route from Milton station to the coal staithes. The line was to be leased by Lord Carlisle to Thompsons the colliery managers for 50 years.

On 8th July 1836 the new branch line to Brampton was finally completed and formally opened 5 days later. Over a thousand people gathered to celebrate the occasion. Two locomotives coupled together hauled a train of 23 wagons and carriages from Kirkhouse to Brampton. Some of the wagons were laden with coal, some had been temporarily converted to coaches with seats for VIPs and guests, whilst another contained *"an excellent band festooned with banners"*. The 0-4-0 engine at the head of the train was Lord Carlisle's locomotive the "Gilsland", which was coupled up to a second locomotive called "Atlas":

"… of very beautiful construction and is calculated for working at a great speed … they moved off amidst the enthusiastic cheers of the assembled multitude, responded to with equal enthusiasm by those in the carriages, the discharges of artillery, the firing of guns, the merry music of the bands and the waving of colours."

Carlisle Journal, July, 1836

On arrival at the opening ceremony, James Thompson proudly announced that on the journey they had travelled at 20 miles per hour. There was music, flags and the firing of a cannon to mark the occasion, followed by a hearty meal in gaily decorated tents, and a dance.

LORD CARLISLE'S RAILWAY.—We have been disappointed by the non-arrival of the report, which a correspondent had promised to furnish to us, of the opening of Lord Carlisle's Railway from Midgeholm, by Milton, to the coal-staiths at Brampton. The day was observed as a complete holyday by all the neighbourhood. The Atlas and Gilsland locomotive engines were employed on the occasion, and started from Kirkhouse, the residence of Mr. James Thompson, Lord Carlisle's principal colliery agent, about half-past 11 in the morning, with a long train of carriages filled with spectators, and accompanied with music and flags, and amidst the firing of cannon. The procession proceeded to the coal-staiths at Brampton, where refreshment was provided, and then returned in the same order. At Kirkhouse a large tent was set out for the accommodation of the work people and visitors and an ample supply of provisions was provided. About a thousand persons sat down to dinner under the presidency of Mr. John Ramshay, and mirth and good fellowship were kept up till a late hour. In another tent tea was provided for the females, and in the evening a dance was struck up. The whole went off remarkably well; and too much credit cannot be given to Mr. Thompson for the admirable completeness of all the arrangements.

Carlisle Journal, July 16, 1836

Chapter 6

BUT, TROUBLE RIGHT FROM THE START

Soon after the clamour and excitement of the opening celebrations had died away, the mood changed rapidly. After a matter of weeks, it was found that the new track was not strong enough to support the heavy locomotives "Gilsland" and "Atlas". The immense disappointment of local people was matched by the frustration of the line operators who had to make the painful and unpopular decision to withdraw the locomotives and to replace them with …**horses!**

The local population, finding that they had been given a new modern branch railway line but were now served by an old fashioned horse drawn service, felt cheated and that they deserved better.

Three carriages called "Dandies" were commissioned for the horse drawn service and bore the names of *Black Diamond*, *Mountaineer* and *Experiment*. They were very basic – open to the air but with iron poles on each corner to suspend a tarpaulin canopy and curtains. A Brampton shopkeeper in 1837 claimed that these carriages had been converted from redundant stage coaches by Messrs Thompsons.

Dandy Carriage.

The journey took twenty minutes and the price of a one way ticket was three pence. A brass "token" could also be purchased in advance which when handed over to the conductor was accepted as an alternative to the ticket.

> You remember the old tickets for the Dandy line? They were substantial pieces of brass, which were purchased at the old Newcastle Station on the London Road when you took your ticket for Brampton. These were, however, done away with subsequently.

As before, the horse was used to pull the Dandy coach from Milton station along the branch line for the first three quarters of a mile until the final downhill section, where the horse was removed, put onto a special cart at the rear, the two coaches being allowed to run – fed by gravity until it approached the coal staith whereupon the driver George Menzies of Brampton, locally known as George Mingins, would bring it to a halt. There is no evidence to show that "buffers" were in place to stop the carriage but merely a mound of earth!

There was much dissatisfaction with what the travelling public considered to be a very poor service. A Brampton shopkeeper described the carriages as:

"a small wagon for passengers, and in it of course, all sorts of individuals, saints and sinners, drunk and sober, pious and profane, are all huddled together to the consequent disgust of the majority."

It was, none-the-less, heavily used, being the only means of getting to and from Milton station to Brampton Town.

In 1875, a serious "near miss" took place involving a full load of 80 passengers in the four Dandy carriages drawn by a horse, with Joseph Bell the conductor in charge.

For some strange reason passenger Daniel Graham, a pitman from Talkin, took it into his head that it would be quite simple to uncouple the three rearmost carriages from the first whilst travelling along the line. This he did and as the horse, conductor and first carriage continued rather more quickly because of the lessened load, it soon became obvious to Mr Bell that something was wrong particularly as he heard screaming from the rear of the train. Bringing the horse to a halt, Mr Bell then noticed the three remaining carriages fully laden with passengers rapidly advancing under their own momentum and about to crash into the first carriage and horse. Luckily Mr Bell was able to jump onto the careering carriages and apply the brake just in time to avoid a collision.

Petty Sessions.

BRAMPTON.—MONDAY, NOV. 1.

(Before G. J. Johnson, Esq., and Dr. Armstrong.)

THE TAMPERING WITH "DANDY" COUPLINGS.— Daniel Graham, pitman, Havanna, near Talkin, was brought up in custody charged with having, on Saturday night last, between seven and eight o'clock, uncoupled two carriages travelling on the tramway between Milton Station and Brampton.—Joseph Bell, conductor, stated that on the night in question he was in charge of four carriages containing 80 passengers, from Milton to Brampton. Shortly after leaving Milton Station, the horse which he was driving started forward and he felt there was not so much weight behind as when they started. He also heard screams from the hindmost carriages. With difficulty he stopped the horse and ran back and met the three last carriages coming by themselves towards the first one. With assistance he stopped the three carriages, and got them coupled to the others and took them to Brampton without any damage being done. Defendant was sitting on the hind part of the first carriage, and was pointed out to him as the man who had uncoupled the waggons. In consequence he gave the prisoner in charge of a policeman who was on one of the carriages.—Jane Thompson and ——— Hetherington, passengers by the "dandy" saw the defendant attempting to uncouple the waggons. They told him two or three times not to do it, but he persisted and took the coupling bolt out and the carriages separated, whereupon they screamed. The conductor came and stopped them. In defence, the defendant said—"I had had a sup and was coming along with the 'dandy' when a man who was in the waggon, said 'There would not be easily uncoupled.' I replied I could do it, and just did it, and am sorry for it."—The Bench inflicted a fine of £2 10s. and 1s. costs.

Many complained that the journey was *"uncomfortable, exposed to the elements, regularly overcrowded, and too expensive"*. Following three years of complaints, Thompsons the lease holders finally agreed to make improvements to the journey and replaced the rolling stock with much improved closed coaches with full protection from the weather, with doors, a "running board" and a step for passengers to climb on board more easily and painted in full livery:

> *"The peculiar construction of the car will be noticed with the open end seats and central compartment with unglazed windows. Small circular wooden buffers attached to an ornamental headstock on which the pin and shackle are fastened."*
>
> Locomotive Magazine, 1903

A Dandy Coach at Brampton coal staith.

The line from Milton Station into Brampton Town remained a horse drawn service for the next 40 years, despite very many debates, meetings, protests and petitions.

Brampton people became weary of the outmoded system of travel and wishing for better things, there was continual agitation for change. Peter Burn, the renowned Brampton poet, composed the following poem:

6. BUT, TROUBLE RIGHT FROM THE START

THE "DANDY."

When holidays and school began,
I rode within the little van,
That with and without horses ran,
    And strangely nam'd the "Dandy."

Great changes have been wrought since then;
The Telegraph out-runs the pen,
The Telephone the tongues of men—
    Yet still we have the "Dandy."

Full forty years have had their run;
I've had my share of work and fun,
I've seen strange things "beneath the sun,"
    But nought to match the "Dandy."

Our grand-dames had the old pack-horse;
Then came the dogcart in its course;
Now youngsters mount the iron horse,
    And Brampton runs its "Dandy."

Our town is small: so it will be;
It had—and has—its thousands three;
It talks and dreams "prosperity!"
    Its nightmare is the "Dandy."

The railway leaves us "in the cold,"
Directors name a grievance old,
Are we for ever to be told—
    Your grand-dads chose the "Dandy?"

Let this pervade their money-plan:
Man lives to serve his brother-man!
Then blessing shall replace the ban,—
    The "Train" replace the "Dandy."

Brampton.   PETER BURN.

The illustration above of the Dandy was intended as a light-hearted criticism in which a would-be passenger is attempting to overtake the horse drawn coach.

When George Mingins died in 1879 his obituary referred to him as a man with genial manners, and unvarying courtesy:

BRAMPTON — DEATH OF AN OLD INHABITANT.—On Wednesday last in Farlam churchyard the grave closed over the mortal remains of a well-known and widely esteemed character in the person of George Menzies, or Mingings, better known as "Old George," for many years the driver of the Brampton "dandy." George was born at Coal Fell in 1795, and had thus completed his 84th year. He was a waggonman on the old railway from the Tindale Fell coal pits to Brampton coalstaith for many years; he being one of some 50 or 60 men so employed, each of whom had charge of one waggon and horse. His father took the first waggon down in April, 1799. On the opening of the Newcastle and Carlisle Railway in 1836, George took charge of the tram car running from Milton Station to Brampton, better known as the "dandy," and continued to do so until June 1871, when he retired upon a pension granted to him by his employers, Messrs. M. Thompson and Sons, of Kirkhouse, in whose service he had been since 1805. In March, 1870, a few leading tradesmen in the town hearing that he was about to retire from the management of the dandy, started a subscription which was so popular among all classes of the community that it resulted in the handsome sum of £79 being handed over to him for the use of himself and sister. The presentation took place at the Howard Arms Hotel, Brampton, and was made by the late Mr. Carrick. Owing to his ready wit, genial manners, and unvarying courtesy, George was an especial favourite with commercial travellers and others using the dandy, and for a long series of years he was regarded quite in the light of a "local institution." The death of his sister, who kept house for him for over 40 years at the Coalstaith, and who died only about a month ago at the ripe age of 80, had a marked effect upon him, and his nephew had him removed to Lockerbie, where he died on Monday last, the 23rd inst.

The Dandy coach in the picture below operated on the Old Port Carlisle to Bowness on Solway line and was almost identical to that which operated on Brampton's Dandy line.

Chapter 7

MEETINGS, PROTESTS, PETITIONS, PROPOSALS, COUNTER PROPOSALS... All Come To Nothing

Throughout the 40 year lifespan of the Dandy horse drawn service, there was continual pressure upon rail companies to bring the Newcastle to Carlisle line nearer to Brampton. Much of these efforts were thwarted by the commercial interests of influential land owners and coal merchants:

> *"It is my opinion that Lord Carlisle should not act the way he does in winking at the monopoly of those coal merchants."*
>
> *Mr T.R. Riddell*

The Newcastle and Carlisle Railway Company became absorbed into the bigger North East Railway Company (NER) which was then asked to consider the construction of a proper branch line to Brampton. After some deliberation the NER directors claimed such an extension would be uneconomical.

In 1846 the Glasgow, Dumfries and Carlisle Railway Company proposed a route from Brampton to Carlisle parallel to the Longtown road then to join the 1799 waggonway to Milton station. In the same year The Caledonian Railway Company proposed a similar route.

In 1852 The Glasgow and South Western Railway Company put forward similar proposals followed by a further proposal in 1865 from the Brampton and Longtown Railway Company.

The Brampton and Longtown Railway proposal gained much momentum and a Bill containing all of the plans was presented to and passed by the House of Commons. However when the Bill was presented to the House of Lords for its final approval, it met with severe opposition.

A petition addressed to The Duke of Devonshire requesting his support for the Brampton Longtown Railway Bill had been got up and signed by over 175 tradesmen and important people of Brampton:

To His Grace, The Most Noble The Duke of Devonshire
May it please your Grace:

We the undersignees, householders and tradesmen of the town of Brampton beg respectfully to address your Grace on a subject of vital importance to the trade and general prosperity of this place.

The Newcastle and Carlisle Railway as first projected would have led to a station at Brampton, but through the influence of parties taking a mistaken view of the interests of the town, the course of the line was diverted so that the nearest station is upwards of two miles distant.

The Trade and Market of Brampton have been injured and the town has been placed at a great disadvantage by being thus left destitute of railway accommodation.

By the Brampton and Longtown Railway Bill now pending in the House of Lords, it is proposed to authorise the construction of a railway which will have a station in Brampton and by which the undersigned believe the prosperity of the town and trade of Brampton will be greatly increased.

We therefore respectfully pray that your Grace as trustee of the Earl of Carlisle whose property will be benefitted thereby, will do whatever may be in his powers to assist the Bill in passing through the House of Lords and to encourage the construction of the proposed Brampton and Longtown Railway.

Sadly, the bill met with opposition in the House of Lords. The Duke of Devonshire acting as trustee to the Earl of Carlisle was advised that:

"… as the proposed line will run for a considerable distance alongside the Lord Carlisle Railway in Rowbank Wood, there will be a very great danger from the plantation taking fire from the hot cinders from locomotive engines which is certain to arise.

Also, a difficulty will arrive with the North Eastern Railway by the carrying of Lord Carlisle's minerals over their line at Milton station at present they use that line without charge. If this is made into a public railway, the question will be that the NER will have the power to put in force their 'short tonnage clause' and charge £2 a ton upon all minerals from Lord Carlisle's works for this short distance. This will amount to several thousand pounds in the year.

The railway should not be allowed to pass within 200 yards of farm buildings.

It is difficult to see where the material for the very high embankments will come from – there is insufficient in the area.

No part of the railway should be seen from Naworth."

Once again the interests of the landowners and wealthy coal merchants were able to overrule the ambitions of local people.

Finally The Carlisle, Brampton and Milton Railway Company in 1871 proposed a route from Milton through Rowbank Wood to Aarons town and Hemblesgate, crossing the Tarn road by a bridge of 30 feet span and 15 feet high crossing Paving Brow parallel to Craw Hall then to Moatside with a further bridge of 40 feet span leading to Crooked Holme crossing the River Irthing by a bridge close to Brampton Old Church then on to Carlisle with stations at Irthington, Crosby and Brunstock. The proposal was for a light railway of narrow gauge:

"PROPOSED RAILWAY BETWEEN BRAMPTON AND CARLISLE
The town of Brampton has unfortunately for itself and the immediate vicinity been left out in the cold by the present railway system. Knowing the serious effects of this unfortunate isolation many projects have been

suggested from time to time for increasing the means of communication, but though some were launched with fair prospects and under favourable auspices, all from one cause or another were nipped in the bud and had to be abandoned. Another scheme is now in embryo for the better development of the local traffic, widely different in its details from any yet brought before the public. Its promoters suggest a single line of railway leaving Brampton on the north side and having intermediate stations near Irthington, Crosby and Brunstock. The gauge is to be 3 feet and the rolling stock and other accessories are to be of a light though substantial character."

Carlisle Journal, July, 1871

By October of that year, surveying of the proposed route was complete and arrangements made to hold a public consultation meeting.

Meanwhile ! ! … the local gentry and landowners, the very people that the proposed railway wished to attract, were busy making a plan of their own – to attempt to persuade the North Eastern Railway Company to extend the Dandy line a further 700 yards right into the centre of Brampton's Market Place. Mr Ramshay, Lord Carlisle's agent at a public meeting rubbished the proposed narrow gauge single track railway plans of the Carlisle and Brampton Milton Railway referring to it as "The Tom Thumb" railway. He argued successfully that the Irthington – Brunstock route would not provide communication with the North East and since it was to be of a different gauge then there would be much transferring and handling of goods.

The planners of the Brampton- Irthington- Brunstock line retaliated by proposing to extend their line to Milton which would then connect with the North East traffic. But by February 1872 the plans for this narrow gauge route were abandoned.

Despite all of these proposed schemes, the Dandy line plodded its way between the coal staithes and Milton regardless of the feelings now mounting against it. Great political capital was made by blaming those responsible for the original routing of the Dandy line. Some blamed the Newcastle and Carlisle Railway Company for having no desire to serve Brampton at all; others blamed Lord Carlisle who benefitted most by transfer of his coal at the

7. MEETINGS, PROTESTS, PETITIONS, PROPOSALS, COUNTER PROPOSALS...

intersection of the colliery line with the main Newcastle to Carlisle line, and, by allowing Thompsons who leased the Dandy line to only sell coal from the Naworth Colliery at the coal staithes.

Shopkeepers opposed the whole idea of having railways anywhere near Brampton believing that local trade would be lost to Carlisle.

Over the 40 years of protests, petitions and meetings the Dandy line was not without incident:

> THE FATAL ACCIDENT AT BRAMPTON — ROBBERY FROM THE INJURED MAN —An adjourned inquest was held at Brampton on Monday last, to ascertain the particulars of the death of George Little, joiner, South Shields, son of the late Dr. Little, of Mallsburn, Stapleton. It seems the deceased had been on a visit to his friends in the neighbourhood of Brampton, and left for home by the tramway on the evening of Wednesday the 11th, being Brampton hiring day. On that occasion there was an unusual number of passengers, and the deceased remained for the last conveyance, which was a waggon, chiefly for taking luggage. On this waggon was one plank for people to sit upon, and it was fully occupied. Little went and sat on the buffer in front, and though warned of the danger of his position by the conductor, he persisted in keeping his place. When about halfway to the railway station deceased fell from the buffer, and both wheels passed over his thighs. In falling he clutched at a female, and pulled her off into the middle of the tramway, where the waggon passed over her, and did no injury. The inquest has been further adjourned for the evidence of the woman, who was dragged off, and had such a miraculous escape. During the time Little lay in great agony at the coalstaith, he was robbed of his watch, purse, and other things. Mary Ann Hordon, hawker, East Tower Street, Carlisle, was apprehended, and has since been committed to take her trial at the sessions for the offence.

Mary Ann Hordon a 39 year old hawker, was sentenced to six months imprisonment with hard labour, having been found guilty of stealing this unfortunate man's watch; purse containing £2.10s; pocket book and other articles as he lay severely injured.

Letters to the Carlisle Journal argued for a better rail link for Brampton rather than a new church:

> **A NEW CHURCH OR A TRAMWAY FOR BRAMPTON?**
>
> TO THE EDITOR OF THE CARLISLE JOURNAL.
>
> Sir,—Some talk has just arisen concerning the former, for which, it is said, a donation of money from Naworth, and one of land from the Hill, may be relied upon.
>
> As there is much to be said against the idea I would observe that the present church is not 50 years old, has pews covering two-thirds of the floor, a gallery above the other one-third, is ample in every respect for the diminished congregation, and more than befitting the deformity and condition of the town. The newly come vicar has had the pulpit removed from front of the altar, with a view to his being fully heard, but in vain, and until that pulpit is set up in the centre of south wall, as formerly, the service cannot be said to be within audibility.
>
> As no spirit of Solomon hovers here, nor is likely to guide observation to what is infinitely more needed than a modern church, I would mention
>
> 1st. That we have ways, streets, and passages, that beggar description for badness and other rude defects, obliging pedestrians to walk side by side, and with horses, cattle, &c.
>
> 2nd. That we are a shunted town, and will decay further till we have a tramway from the North Eastern Railway Station at Milton into the town.
>
> This 1½ mile tramway could be most easily effected on the Castle Carrock road and Brewery Lane. Passengers could thus come to and go from the town by every train between Newcastle and Carlisle.
>
> Such, sir, is the task I propose instead of the idle injudicious idea of a better church. Let us approximate to that state of railway intercourse of which we were robbed by ignorance, and endeavour to restore the traffic of former days.
>
> A BRAMPTONIAN.
>
> 29th August, 1874.

In 1875, the protestors suggested that the North Eastern Railway should construct a new branch line into Brampton and this was brought before Sir J. Pease and Sir Harcourt Johnstone. A deputation was arranged with the Directors of the NER board – but to no avail; the answer came back:

> *"I am now desired to say that after careful consideration, the Board directors are not able to come to the conclusion that it is desirable for this company to undertake the construction of the branch line as proposed."*

In fact, at a later enquiry it was discovered that in 1876 Thompsons had made a proposal to the Trustees of Lord Carlisle to contribute £4000 towards the cost of extending the Dandy line into the centre of Brampton, provided that the Earl of Carlisle was willing to match with a further sum of £3000. The Earl refused, so the plan was dropped. However, as the dissatisfaction continued to grow, Messrs Thompsons, for one day on the 13th November 1878, borrowed three NER carriages to convey passengers over their "Dandy" line hauled by a steam locomotive! The occasion provided renewed enthusiasm to secure a steam passenger service into Brampton.

> **BRAMPTON TRAMWAY AND RAILWAY STATION.**
>
> TO THE EDITOR OF THE CARLISLE PATRIOT.
>
> SIR,—It was cheering to see a locomotive engine attached to three North-Eastern Railway Company carriages on Wednesday last taking passengers to and from the Coal Hole and railway station. It is quite time something was done to improve the most miserable tramway in existence, and to do away with the bogie-waggon carriages that have been in use over 35 years, and actually to charge 3d per passenger each way for a mile and a half. The carrying of passengers in waggons on deal planks last agricultural show day was a disgrace, when sufficient carriages could have been got from the railway company. The Agricultural Committee could not but feel indignant at such conduct in so treating a respectable company of gentlemen and ladies attending one of the best agricultural shows in Cumberland. The committee deserve all praise for their energy in bringing to the show such a large company and successful issue. I have made it my duty to inquire carefully why the North-Eastern Railway Company have not made Brampton (Milton) station so comfortable and convenient as their other stations on the Newcastle and Carlisle section, which has been done at other stations of much less importance. I find that the Railway Company's surveyors have been twice from York at Brampton with plans to improve the station, but had been met with difficulties in connection with Lord Carlisle's lessees and agents. The fact of this being the only station on the Newcastle and Carlisle section not in order speaks for itself of the difficulties the Railway Company have to grapple with. If the energetic Agricultural Committee and the inhabitants of Brampton and district would act independently, they would suggest to the North-Eastern Railway Company to remove the station to Brampton Fell Gates, or that the heirs of Lord Carlisle's estate and influential gentlemen and proprietors of Brampton would come forward and offer to the North-Eastern Railway Company money on debenture stock, at a reasonable rate of interest for perpetuity—to extend the tramway, there might be a hope of Brampton yet being saved from ruin.—Yours, &c.,   PROSPERITY.

Carlisle Journal, 1878

In March of that year a letter summarising the views of the travelling public of the Dandy service opened up new efforts to bring about improvements:

Sir,

What crime have the people of Brampton, or their forefathers, committed that they and their visitors should be condemned to such severe punishment on either entering or leaving their ancient market town? The slave trade is acquainted with the horrors of the "middle passage" – now the unfortunate inhabitants of Brampton have their middle passage along a tramway which has been carefully kept at a most inconvenient distance from the town and in a primitive kind of carriage called "the Dandy". It is of no use now going back to the record of mingled prejudice and blunder which perversely sent the main line of railway from its natural and easy route between the valley of Eden and that of the Irthing, past a thriving market town to a distance of two miles through a most expensive cutting past no place at all. If the station is to be two miles off, that is no reason why it should not be comfortable and safe with suitable attention and accommodation in every way. If the Brampton people must travel by the tramway their journey should not be a torture. They have a right to expect sufficient facilities, roomy and wholesome carriages, a division of classes, and civility from those in charge. How far all these conditions are from being fulfilled, no one who has travelled by rail to Brampton needs to be told. The Brampton platform is low and to step down onto it is awkward and hazardous – particularly to ladies and elderly people. There is scarcely a feature of a proper station that is not conspicuous by its absence. There is no covering, so that passengers remain in the open air, exposed to wind, rain, snow, cold and dust. The Directors may enjoy a monopoly, but they should not utterly ignore their responsibilities to the public. No description in words can fully bring out the utter unsuitability of the Dandy for the purpose it has been expected to do. It is too small in every way. There is no proper place for luggage and, as frequently happens, people cannot be squeezed any closer inside, in the front and at the back, they have to stand clustering around the steps at considerable hazard to their limbs. If in spite of all the squeezing, there is neither sitting nor standing room left, or a gentleman makes way for a lady, so that some passengers are compelled to walk, they are rudely told that they will have to pay all the same. There is no division of classes – a well dressed lady may find herself next to a chimney sweep or to a navvy covered with the dirt of his honourable toil.

AN AGGRIEVED TRAVELLER, 22 March, 1878

A further scathing report appeared in the Carlisle Journal the following week:

Sir,

I ask permission to add my testimony to that of 'An aggrieved traveller' as to the utterly disgraceful condition of matters at what is called Brampton Station. … to have to be huddled into one little pen like so many sheep, and bear the stew and stench of the bibulous devotees with their lewdness and ribaldry was to me so terrible. The special circumstance which haunts my memory happened on a busy night when for venturing to suggest to a half drunken 'haveral' that four stout persons were enough for the end ledge of the Dandy, I had a narrow escape from a thrashing. The Dandy was something between a coal cart and a railway manure vehicle, and into these were crammed a score or two of people, male and female – the males being mostly in that condition known in the vernacular as 'splashed'. The 'Dandy' must be abolished, and some better means of getting into town and out of it must be secured.

F. Chester, 25 March, 1878

Finally a public meeting was called for the 20th April 1880 at The Howard Arms Hotel.

> **BRAMPTON RAILWAY ACCOMMODATION.**
> A PUBLIC MEETING will be held in the HOWARD ARMS ASSEMBLY ROOM, BRAMPTON, on TUESDAY, the 20th APRIL, 1880, at Two o'Clock in the Afternoon, for the purpose of "Considering the Present Railway Accommodation to the Town, and the course to be adopted for improving the same."
> All interested are invited to attend.
> JOHN CARRICK, Hon. Secretary.

The meeting was attended by over 150 people with the purpose of deciding what further action should be taken. Much criticism came from the public:

"The district is suffering a great inconvenience from the want of a proper railway accommodation for the town.

Imagine a traveller or visitor coming to Brampton by the Newcastle and Carlisle Railway. He has paid a ticket for, and reaches Brampton station to find that it is not Brampton but Milton – this is misleading.

He opens the door of his carriage and prepares to step out – if he does not look out he will tumble; if he does look out he will find there is a perilous descent to be gone through before he reaches the ground – the platform is dangerously low.

There is no shelter so people waiting for the train or for a connection to arrive must stand uncovered in the open air, in wind, rain and snow and sleet.

In order to reach Brampton he must go by the Dandy – a remarkable vehicle where the compartments are filled with baggage as well as passengers.

The vehicle has no cushions – travellers who are lucky enough to get inside being crushed together – ladies, gentlemen and workmen in working dress.

If he is a stranger and wears a top hat the chances are that it will be crushed, and if the person be a lady and has a fine dress on, the chances are that she will go away with a worse temper than she came.

Although smoking is not allowed this is not followed.

There are usually a greater number of passengers than can be accommodated – even on normal days the vehicle is usually full with others hanging precariously on the outside.

Part way through the journey the imaginary traveller now finds that the horse is taken off, and that he is now conveyed by some unseen power … gravitation, and if he is of an inquiring mind no doubt will question what would be the result if the brake should fail.

After he has got to the end of the Dandy line and had paid his three pence, he naturally expects that he has arrived at his journey's end, but unfortunate man! He finds he has got another mile to walk with baggage perhaps through rain and dirt and sludge to the town."

7. MEETINGS, PROTESTS, PETITIONS, PROPOSALS, COUNTER PROPOSALS...

By the end of the meeting, it was agreed that the accommodation for Brampton and surrounding district was inadequate in every respect, and that the North Eastern Railway Company be requested to meet a deputation of the inhabitants of Brampton to discuss the question of railway accommodation for the town.

The socio-political climate at this time was one of wealth creation by rich landowners, tradesmen and politicians on the one hand and the desire of ordinary working folk on the other hand, who felt that they were left out in the cold and deserved better living standards. The only people who were qualified to vote in parliamentary elections were landowners and property owners. This particular group had vested interests in gaining wealth and most likely therefore wished to protect any monopoly that gave them advantage. Those who were not property owners were therefore in a weak position, unable to influence members of parliament, or employers.

The Parliamentary Act in 1829 for the construction of the Newcastle to Carlisle line contained a clause whereby the directors were bound down not to afford any facilities to the public for obtaining coal, lime or minerals other than those produced by the pits of the Naworth estate, thus giving Lord Carlisle a monopoly of such trade.

Thompsons, the sole operator of the Brampton branch line were vehemently opposed to any other operator using "their" line. Also, in a letter from "Prosperity" some clues appear to lay the blame on Thompsons the leaseholders:

"I have made it my duty to inquire carefully why the North Eastern Railway has not made Milton Station so comfortable and convenient as their other stations on the Newcastle to Carlisle line which has been done at other stations of lesser importance. I find that the railway's surveyors have been twice from York at Brampton with plans to improve the station but had met with difficulties in connection with Lord Carlisle's lessees and agents."
PROSPERITY Carlisle Journal, 19 November, 1878

Similarly, Brampton tradesmen's opposition to the railway developments were based on their fear of competition from shops and businesses in Carlisle. Their strongly held view was that their trade would be lost if their present customers could travel to Carlisle by rail. Brampton tradesmen and shopkeepers equally wished to protect their monopoly to safeguard their future.

Politicians, keen to hold on to their seat in parliament, were acutely aware of the need to support land and property owners, who at that stage were the only people eligible to vote.

Against this background of monopoly and privilege a new age of Liberalism and reform was about to dawn. In 1869 the first struggles to seek a fairer society began in Brampton as elsewhere. At first the people of Brampton and neighbourhood appeared indifferent, but when they began to hear of the ruinous influence of monopoly, making itself felt in many devious and unsuspected ways, hampering any enterprise started by ordinary folk they roused from their complacency. By 1880, the liberals made sweeping gains across the country heralding a period of reform, free trade and the end to monopoly and privilege.

Chapter 8

A NEW DAWN BREAKS OVER THE FUTURE FOR BRAMPTON'S RAILWAY FACILITIES?

The Directors of the North Eastern Railway Company appear to have acquiesced under the pressure from the petitions, protests and presentations of the inhabitants of Brampton and agreed to make some improvements both to Milton Station, the track itself and to Brampton coal staithes. Nine months after the 1880 public meeting in the Howard Arms, the NER began work on improvements.

The platform at Milton station was raised 2½ feet higher to coincide with the exit from the Dandy coach. New waiting rooms and accommodation for first and second class passengers with toilets and a porters room now brought this station up to the standard of most others on the Newcastle to Carlisle Line. At the Brampton terminus there were extensions and a new platform.

But, the great sticking point to improving the branch into Brampton town via the Dandy was that Thompsons who were the lease owners of the line would not agree to sharing it with any other operator. Also, Lord Carlisle as owner of the land over which the line travelled, continued to insist – by lease and by the original act of Parliament – that the only coal and lime to be carried over the line was to be that from his Naworth collieries. This had secured for Lord Carlisle a monopoly of the sale of coal in Brampton, and for Thompsons it had secured the monopoly of use of the line for themselves. Unfortunately, therefore, because of the above restrictions, the Dandy coach had to remain the only method of passenger transport from Milton station to Brampton Town. Much political pressure was now brought upon the monopolists to ease the restrictions, and finally on the 4th July 1881, the hopes and ambitions of Brampton people came to part fruition when the old one-horse Dandy after 45 years of service was finally replaced by a…

Steam Locomotive!

This was a gigantic leap forward for travellers.

> **THE BRAMPTON RAILWAY.**
> Yesterday morning the old one-horse "Dandy" which has accommodated the railway traffic between Brampton and Milton for the last forty-five years, and has afforded a subject for much criticism, facetious or seriously indignant, as the case might be, for many years, disappeared from the scene, and was superseded by a powerful tank locomotive engine, made by Messrs. Neilson and Co., of Glasgow, drawing a couple of new and comfortable modern carriages, containing first and third-class compartments, and capable of accommodating about fifty passengers.

The locomotive was a four-wheeled tank engine no. 2738 bought from Neilson and Co. Ltd Glasgow and named "Dandie Dinmont", painted in green.

Not only was a new locomotive provided but also three new very comfortable passenger carriages were bought from the London and North Western Railway to provide first, second and third class accommodation totalling 50 seats.

8. A NEW DAWN BREAKS OVER THE FUTURE FOR BRAMPTON'S RAILWAY FACILITIES?

Dandie Dinmont, tank engine no. 2738.

Dandie Dinmont 0-4-0Toc (N2738/81) built for Thompsons for use specifically on the passenger traffic between Brampton staith and the N. & C. line station at Milton (Brampton Junction). Here it is depicted with its train of ex-L.N.W.R. carriages in 1881 at the staith. (B. Webb)

Scene at Brampton Town Station in about 1885. The 0-4-0 side tank Dandie Dinmont, built by Neilson's in 1881 specially for the steam passenger service, waits with two of the three ex-L.N.W.R. four-wheeled coaches for the signal to proceed on another trip to Brampton Junction. The driver seems most likely to be William Stobbart snr., and the guard, Thomas Foster, is standing beside the end carriage (second from left). (Mrs T.E. Dixon)

A scene in the mid-1800s showing Dandie Dinmont climbing away from Brampton coal staith over the 1836 skew arch with a two-coach train for Brampton Junction. (Sid Barnes)

8. A NEW DAWN BREAKS OVER THE FUTURE FOR BRAMPTON'S RAILWAY FACILITIES?

The local press were delighted with the improvements:

"Messrs Thompsons, without solicitation, have undertaken to provide a steam engine and suitable carriages for use on Lord Carlisle's line of which they are lessees."

Line drawing of Dandie Dinmont.

Compared with the 20 minute horse drawn journey pulling one coach, the locomotive Dandie Dinmont pulling three coaches achieved the journey in three minutes. Trustees of Lord Carlisle announced their satisfaction with the improvements:

"The carriages which Mr Thompson has put on are excellent in every respect – the 3rd Class is so good that the first class might be dispensed with – If the Brampton people are not satisfied now with the accommodation given, they may make their own railway."

Three generations of the Stobbart family of Hallbankgate served on the footplate of the Dandie Dinmont. Mr William Stobbart and his son John were driver and fireman and later, grandson William followed the family tradition as fireman.

The old horse-drawn Dandy made its last trip at 10.30 a.m on the 4th July 1881 and soon afterwards the Dandie Dinmont, drawing a train bedecked with flowers and evergreens, contained a large party of VIPs and many locals who had campaigned for the improvements and made its way to Brampton town. Improvements were also made at the coal staith end of the line. A proper platform was built, a waiting room and a new approach road while the line itself was relaid with steel rails on wooden sleepers. Thompsons even considered the possibility of extending the line further into the town!

Again, the new railway was not without problems. In 1886 a great storm and gale descended upon Brampton causing much damage:

"At Brampton, the storm did considerable damage to houses and property. The store room of the Rifle Ranges was unroofed; the new goods shed at Milton Station sustained a deal of injury; A serious accident doubtless the result of the storm, occurred on the Dandy Line. Mr William Laidler of Hemblesgate farm had a number of sheep in one of the fields running alongside the railway, but the gate had been blown open by the violence of the wind. Several of the sheep had strayed on the line and as the train which leaves the coal staithes at 6.30 pm was proceeding to Brampton Station, it ran into them killing six and injuring four others."

Carlisle Journal, February, 1886

> SERIOUS ACCIDENT NEAR BRAMPTON STATION.—A serious accident befel James Brown, quarryman, Talkin, on Saturday evening last. As the "Dandy Dinmont" was running to meet the 9 p.m. train due from Carlisle, the engine driver and guard thought they observed something on the line, about one hundred yards from Brampton Station. On arriving at the station they took a lamp, and proceeded to the place, where they found Brown lying in a sad state, his left arm being taken off between the elbow and wrist, whilst a portion of his left foot was severely crushed. He was speedily conveyed to Brampton Station, where temporary bandages were applied by Mr. Wilson, the station-master, who afterwards had the injured man removed to Carlisle Infirmary. Brown, who had been at Carlisle hiring, had evidently strayed upon the branch line instead of proceeding home, and had been run over by the train running to Brampton Coal Staith.

Carlisle Journal, 1884

Chapter 9

THE "NEW DAWN" TURNS INTO AN "EARLY SUNSET"

Unfortunately the euphoria of the new arrangements was to last only ten years. In 1890 Thompsons' lease of the line was due to be renewed and before this was to take place, Lady Carlisle insisted upon a survey and inspection of the system by a Board of Trade Inspector.

Thompsons secretly favoured the prospect of working the line exclusively for coal traffic which generated a clear profit; whilst the passenger service created a loss, and once the line was found unfit for passengers, Thompsons would be free of their obligation to provide for passengers, but able to continue with the profitable coal traffic alone.

Lady Rosalind, on the other hand wished for the line to be placed in the hands of the North Eastern Railway who hopefully would respect the advice from the Board of Trade Inspector and carry out the improvements, so that the future of the line for the people of Brampton would be secure.

Major-General Hutchinson, Inspector of Railways for The Board of Trade duly visited the line, and his report was not good news: the inspector identified that this was a single line on which there were 2 trains simultaneously working a passenger service in opposite directions without any signalling system; no staff, and a gradient of 1 in 30 to be negotiated without a continuous braking system! The inspector's recommendations included:

1. At the Brampton Town terminus all sidings to be improved with throw off points; the sharp curve near the platform to have a check rail and the steps at the end of the platform to be changed to a ramp.
2. The loop sidings at both ends of the line to be removed.
3. All points to be fitted with double connecting rods.
4. Fencing to be repaired.
5. Mile posts and gradient boards to be erected.
6. Locomotives to have six wheels and both it and the carriages to be fitted with continuous and automatic braking system.

The list of recommendations from the Inspector was handed to Thompsons, the lease holders, who declared that the cost of making such improvements would be uneconomical for them, but were not opposed to the NER taking possession of the line and carrying out the improvements.

The NER at first did not discount the prospect of investing in the line to meet the inspector's recommendations, and taking over possession of the line – but it was Thompsons' insistence that they would retain running powers over the line for their coal traffic that led to all negotiations breaking down.

To the dismay of Lady Carlisle and the Brampton inhabitants, the North Eastern Railway decided not to take possession of the line and Thompsons duly announced in The Carlisle Journal that the passenger service to Brampton from Milton was to be withdrawn.

> BRAMPTON RAILWAY.
> NOTICE IS HEREBY GIVEN, that after the Expiration of the Present Month, we shall CEASE to CONVEY PASSENGERS between BRAMPTON JUNCTION and BRAMPTON COALSTAITH
> THOMPSON & SON.
> Kirkhouse, April 16th, 1890.

9. THE "NEW DAWN" TURNS INTO AN "EARLY SUNSET"

> THE LAST OF THE BRAMPTON "DANDY."—Our advertising columns to-day contain an announcement which will be very unpleasant news to the people of Brampton. It is announced that after the expiration of the present month the "Dandy" on the Brampton Railway will cease to convey passengers. A service of coaches from the Station to the town is talked of, but nothing definite has yet been decided upon.

Thompsons' "hidden agenda" to have the loss making passenger service withdrawn whilst retaining the profit making mineral traffic had been achieved.

Brampton townspeople were once more disappointed and again, petitions were got together to encourage the North Eastern Railway company to reconsider taking over the line from Thompsons.

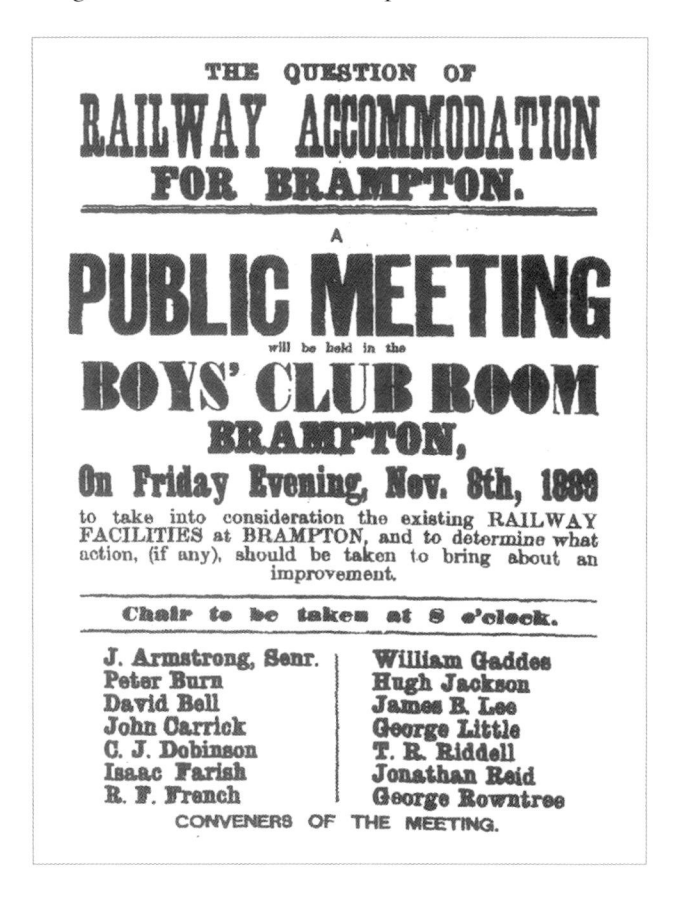

> THE QUESTION OF
> **RAILWAY ACCOMMODATION FOR BRAMPTON.**
> A
> **PUBLIC MEETING**
> will be held in the
> **BOYS' CLUB ROOM BRAMPTON,**
> On Friday Evening, Nov. 8th, 1889
> to take into consideration the existing RAILWAY FACILITIES at BRAMPTON, and to determine what action, (if any), should be taken to bring about an improvement.
>
> Chair to be taken at 8 o'clock.
>
> | | |
> |---|---|
> | J. Armstrong, Senr. | William Gaddes |
> | Peter Burn | Hugh Jackson |
> | David Bell | James B. Lee |
> | John Carrick | George Little |
> | C. J. Dobinson | T. R. Riddell |
> | Isaac Farish | Jonathan Reid |
> | R. F. French | George Rowntree |
>
> CONVENERS OF THE MEETING.

Meanwhile, Thompsons, keen to ensure that the line be kept for their coal traffic, began to heap further demands and conditions if the NER were to take over the line. In late March, Thompsons issued instructions that in the event of NER pursuing their intention to take over the line, then Thompsons should be paid the value of all the rails and sleepers thereon, and also the value of the station, platform and carriage sheds.

Unfortunately for the Bramptonians, the directors of NER were determined not to do anything to help resurrect the line since it was more remunerative for them to have goods carried from Milton station into Brampton by lorry rather than the branch line.

> The North Eastern Railway Company seem determined not to do anything to help Brampton out of the difficulty in which it has been placed by the stoppage of the Dandy. Indeed, they have discovered that it is more remunerative to them to carry goods from the Junction to Brampton by lorry than by rail, because they get such good prices for the work. The latest idea of the Bramptonians, or rather of the Committee who have had charge of the matter, was that a private company should be formed to keep the Dandy line, or some substitute for it, in good order, if the railway company would work the traffic. The directors have, however, declined to adopt the proposal. Those Bramptonians, therefore, who prefer the present mode of conveyance between the Junction and the town to the old "Dandy" system are likely to enjoy it for a long time to come. They have only tried it in summer. I wonder if it will be equally delightful in winter.

Once more, to everyone's dismay, profit was considered more important to the owners and leaseholders rather than providing a decent passenger service for the local inhabitants. Meanwhile, in the absence of a rail passenger service, Joe Elliot, a local entrepreneur started up a horse bus service from Brampton Junction directly into the town centre of Brampton by road and was known as "Joe the bus".

*Above: Joe Elliot's bus passing below the now redundant Dandy line bridge.
Left: Joe Elliot's bus.*

The fare was one penny from the town centre to the Brampton Junction station, compared to the three penny fare by the former Dandy line which stopped at the coal staithes – so although returning to a horse-drawn service was seen as a retrograde step, it was none-the-less greatly valued as it was both less expensive and provided a service right into the centre of Brampton. This service lasted for the next 38 years.

Chapter 10

LADY ROSALIND HOWARD TO THE RESCUE

The Howards of Naworth, being ardent Liberals, and with influential connections to the new London Parliament which had embarked on a campaign of reform, began to soften their attitude to monopoly and wealth generation in favour of helping to improve the lot of the working classes. Lady Rosalind in particular was seen as a passionate philanthropist and attended many meetings to promote fairness in society.

By 1890, Thompsons' leasehold of the Brampton branch line was due to expire and new arrangements were being considered.

Lady Rosalind took up the initiative of reopening the line to passengers. She wrote to the Directors of North Eastern Railway Company:

> *"Would the Directors of NER view the question in a more favourable light if the existing railway from Brampton junction to the coal staith were to be GIVEN to them and not sold? I have personally always been of the opinion that if only the NER would work this little branch line, no sum of money would be asked by Lord Carlisle. If Lord Carlisle can facilitate an arrangement by ceding the line free of cost – it shall be done."*

Unfortunately again this offer was rejected.

In 1891, The Brampton Railway Extension Committee was formed by local tradesmen and Councillors with the intention of raising enthusiasm for

The Brampton people are once more on the move about the defective railway accommodation from which the town suffers. For fourteen years they have been crying aloud, but nobody would help them out of the slough into which they had fallen in consequence of the short-sighted policy of their ancestors. The North-Eastern Railway Company have been appealed to time after time; but the present system suits the Company well enough. A ton of heavy goods coming from Manchester to Carlisle costs 20s. delivered free in the city. If sent on to Brampton one fourth more is added, namely half-a-crown for railway carriage, and half-a-crown for cartage. As the traffic to Brampton is 8,000 tons a year, about as much more being sent away, it is not difficult to see that the railway company make a very goodly sum out of the present arrangement. They have the monopoly and they are quite content with it. We are not sanguine, therefore, that the Company will, under these circumstances, give any better answer than they did in 1875 and in 1880. The best hope of the Bramptonians appears to be in the extension and development of the "Dandie" line. The lease has expired or is about to expire, and it is believed that the Earl of Carlisle is very anxious to help the Brampton people in this matter, if he can. The public meeting held on Friday night resolved to memorialise the North Eastern Railway Company to construct a branch into the town; but it is obvious that as we are now half way through November, the month in which parliamentary notices of such undertakings must be given, nothing can be done by them this year. For immediate help the Bramptonians must therefore turn their eyes in a different direction.

THE BRAMPTON RAILWAY QUESTION.

A further reply has been received from the North Eastern Directors in response to the very liberal offer made to them by Lord and Lady Carlisle, in offering the North Eastern Company the present Dandie line as a gift. The Directors are unable to alter their decision, and it is understood that the chief objection to their taking over the line is the opinion of their engineers, who regard the line as unsuitable for their traffic, and that to fit the line to work the North Eastern traffic would involve a considerable outlay.

extending the existing Dandy Line further towards the centre of town and resuming a steam locomotive passenger service. The proposals were to reconsider providing "a light railway service". It was not long before the enthusiasm of this group was dampened by a once more negative response from Messrs Thompsons the leaseholders of the line:

> THE BRAMPTON RAILWAY PROBLEM. — The Brampton Railway Extension Committee are no nearer a solution of the difficult problem that they have in hand. They this week received intimation from Messrs. Thompson, of Kirkhouse, that after very careful investigation into the matter, and inquiries lasting over several months, they cannot see their way to resume the passenger traffic. A meeting of the Committee will probably be held shortly.

In 1904 the proposal for a light railway was still an ambition of the Brampton people and so a public meeting was held in January to rekindle enthusiasm for the project with well researched background information.

Mr Hugh Jackson, Chairman of Brampton Parish Council presented the following information:

1. The average yearly number of passengers carried on the Dandy line was 43,000.
2. This number would certainly be increased if a light railway were to be constructed.
3. The earnings of the Dandy in 1885 had been £607 and in 1889, £605.
4. If a fare of 4d had been charged the revenue would have been £779.
5. To the passenger revenue a further £90 could be added for the transport of parcels and mails.
6. If a fare of 4½d were charged, the estimated revenue would be £952.10s per year.
7. An engineers report indicated that the annual running costs of such a line would be £534 therefore a profit of at least £300 per year could be guaranteed.

8. A capital outlay of £5,000 would be required to construct the line, with shares being available bringing in an annual return to shareholders of 5%.

Mr Arthur Lee added further evidence:

9. That Brampton and district is developing into a pleasure resort – the number of passengers arriving at Brampton Junction in Whitsuntide week recently was no less than **1,197 in one day.**

At the end of the meeting the following resolution was passed:

"That having regard to the interests and the convenience of the inhabitants of the town and the surrounding district, and in view of the great increase that has taken place during the last few years in the excursionists and tourist traffic into this town and neighbourhood, particularly from Newcastle and Sunderland, it is highly desirable that the travelling facilities between Brampton Junction and the town of Brampton should be improved by means of a light railway or otherwise."

Eighteen months of further deliberation by the North Eastern Railway Company and several visits to Brampton by the Principal Officials of the engineering and permanent way departments took place. Meanwhile the patience of the Bramptonians was beginning to wear thin, but members of the Brampton Railway Extension Committee were aware of the need not to put pressure upon the Railway company for fear of being once more rejected:

"We must not force the Railway company so we must exercise patience – these matters take a long time and we have only been in negotiation about twelve months."

1907 – Three years later! – Despite further meetings, discussions and inspections no decision was forthcoming from North Eastern Railway Company. The Brampton Railway Extension Committee reported that negotiations with Lord Carlisle and Thompsons the leaseholders were being carried forward and correspondence with the NER General manager's office in York indicated that it *"would not be possible to start work on the project <u>until the following summer</u>."* Great hopes were therefore attached to this statement by the Bramptonians.

Meanwhile rapid changes were taking place in the principal workings of the Naworth coalfields. During 1893 Midgeholme colliery had become worked out and abandoned, causing much loss of employment.

The situation was eased by the sinking of a new pit at Roachburn, a mile west of Tindal fell. Five years later tragedy struck the Thompson family with the sudden death of Charles at the age of 39. Charles' brother James consequently became the sole lease holder – an extra burden on already over loaded shoulders. Under James' watch, the fortunes of the East Cumberland coalfields began to decline.

In January 1908 disaster struck at Roachburn colliery; water invaded the workings causing substantial loss of life. This tragedy greatly affected James Thompson's health, from which he never recovered. Three months later, the lease of the railway, and collieries was surrendered and the company of Thompson and Sons was dissolved. The future of the collieries and the branch line now looked even more bleak than ever before.

Several long years of negotiations dragged on between the NER, and the Brampton Railway Extension Committee. Offers made, rejected, counter offers made and rejected, each concerned with the fear of financial loss.

However, the redoubtable Lady Rosalind Howard, despite such misfortunes, entered into negotiations with local business interests, and set up a new company – The Naworth Coal Company Ltd. to take over the remnants of the Thompson undertaking and to open up new coal workings at Gairs colliery, high up on the fells of Castle Carrock.

Lady Rosalind took charge of opening up focussed discussions with the North Eastern Railway Company to once more introduce a passenger service to Brampton Town. The NER Directors were impressed – or perhaps more likely dominated by the determination at the no-nonsense attitude of Lady Rosalind and not only agreed to a 50 year lease but also to investing £900 for line and platform improvements, a goods warehouse, new station accommodation at Brampton town, and to crown all this… a new locomotive and rolling stock for…

A New Passenger Service!

The agreement reached in January 1911 included:

1. The railway between Brampton Junction and Brampton coal staith to be leased to the NER for a term of 50 years.
2. The NER to pay a yearly rent of £5 in respect of the railway.
3. The NER to pay Naworth Estates £900 for permanent way materials and platform at Brampton staith.
4. The NER to provide a passenger service between Brampton Junction and the staith and also to work the mineral traffic on the line.
5. The NER to take the coal depot at Brampton at a rent of £60 a year with the company making all necessary alterations and repairs at their own cost.

The final agreement took a further 10 months to sign – but at last Brampton was to have its own passenger service and station.

Chapter 11

THE NEW DAWN HAS FINALLY ARRIVED

Before the Brampton Branch line could be reopened for passenger trains, the NER had to carry out major works. The track bed had to be raised in a narrow part of the Milton Hill cutting by replacing 6,500 cubic yards of earth, and a mile and a half of new track had to be relaid.

The 1836 stone arch over the Brampton to Alston road had to be replaced with a new steel girder bridge deck, strong enough to take the new heavy locomotives. Through the intervention of Lady Rosalind, the Cumberland County Council agreed to contribute £250 towards the cost of the new bridge.

The new station was to be called Brampton Town and was to have a new platform 160 feet long by 15 feet wide built of solid masonry with concrete copings. Waiting rooms, a booking office, and a parcels office were to be of wooden construction and lit by gas.

The new service from Brampton Junction to the town was to be by steam locomotive – a Fletcher 0-4-4 tank engine no. 1089.

There were two coaches – one in front and one behind the engine forming a "push and pull system" so that the train would not need to be turned round.

11. THE NEW DAWN HAS FINALLY ARRIVED

The replacement steel girder bridge deck, strong enough to take the new heavy locomotives.

LIFE IN BRAMPTON WITH THE DANDY

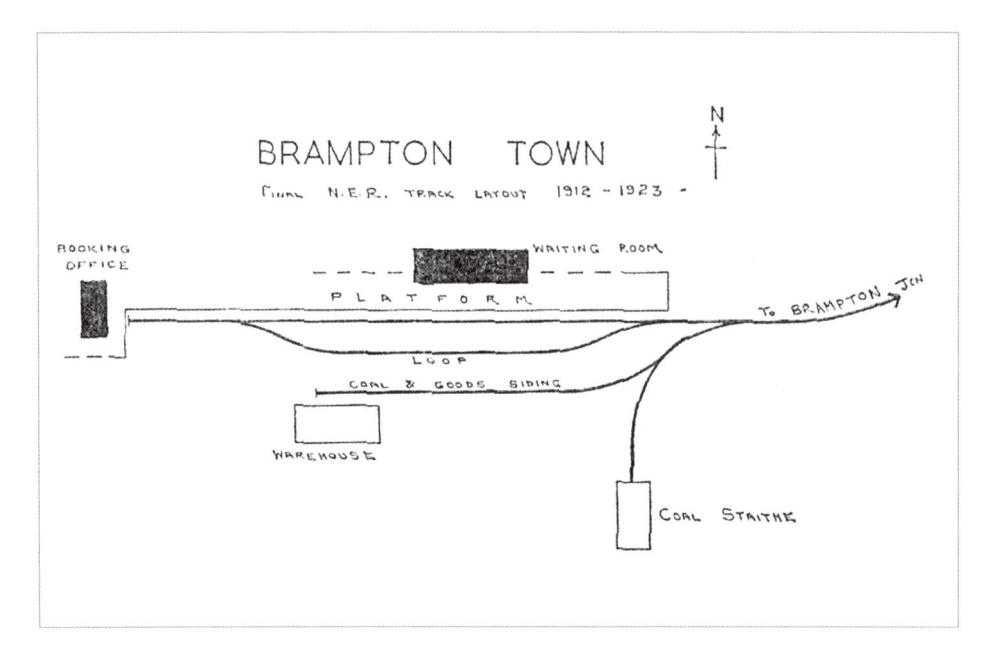

Above: Brampton Town Station track layout.
Right and Below: The Fletcher 0-4-4 tank engine no. 1089 and coach.

11. THE NEW DAWN HAS FINALLY ARRIVED

Lady Cecilia Roberts (light feather boa, centre) and Lady Rosalind (dark feather boa, centre) at the official opening ceremony.

What a truly remarkable day for Brampton was Thursday 31st July 1913! Amidst much pomp and ceremony attended by hundreds of townsfolk, the official opening ceremony was conducted by Lady Cecilia Roberts – a daughter of Lady Rosalind.

Crowds at the official opening ceremony.

11. THE NEW DAWN HAS FINALLY ARRIVED

Crowds at the official opening ceremony.

"Success to the Brampton Branch Railway"

This was truly a gala day for Brampton. Shops closed at 11am, children were given free rides on the railway and sports events held nearby. There were flags and bunting, fireworks, fog horns and much merry making.

After the opening ceremony, the entire party, led by the Brampton Town Band, walked to lunch at The Howard Arms.

It was announced that 28 trains per day would operate to meet all main-line trains, for a fare of 4d single and 6d return – but there was no Sunday service:

```
BRAMPTON JUNCTION and BRAMPTON TOWN.—North Eastern.
                              Week Days only.
        mrn mrn   mrn mrn   mrn    aft aft   aft aft   aft   aft aft   aft    aft
Brampton Junction..dep. 7 40 8 3 .. 8 25 10 4 .. 10 30 .. 2 10 2 40 .. 2 22 50 .. 4 25 .. 4 25 5 40 .. 6 47 .. 7 25
1¼ Brampton Town....arr. 7 45 8 8 .. 8 30 10 9 .. 10 35 .. 2 15 2 45 .. 3 27 3 55 .. 4 30 .. 4 30 5 45 .. 6 52 .. 7 30
                              Week Days only.
        mrn mrn mrn   mrn    mrn    aft    aft aft   aft aft    aft    aft aft    aft
Brampton Town....dep. 7 50 8 12 9 45 .. 10 15 .. 12 13 .. 2 22 .. 3 53 23 .. 4 54 36 .. 5 30 .. 6 35 7 10 .. 7 35
1¼ Brampton Jun. 736..arr. 7 55 8 17 9 50 .. 10 20 .. 12 13 .. 2 27 .. 3 10 3 58 .. 4 10 4 41 .. 5 35 .. 6 40 7 15 .. 7 40
```

One month following the grand opening, the General Committee responsible for managing the new railway arrangements reported that 2,500 passengers were conveyed during the first week and that this traffic seemed to be well maintained. It was estimated that the number of passengers carried on the new line would exceed their estimate. A financial statement was presented indicating that there was a healthy credit balance. The service proved excellent and well supported.

75 years of meetings, raised expectations, dashed hopes, short lived starts, were all now behind them, Brampton bathed in the glory of having at last, an up to date and comfortable railway passenger service … their day had come!

Chapter 12

OH NO, NOT AGAIN?

But again another false dawn was about to break. This delightful service was to last for only ten years. But why?

The end of the line for Brampton's Dandy
Initially the fare was 4d for a single one way journey and this was raised eventually to 7d – making it one of the most expensive fares in England. Competition from Joe Elliot's horse bus at 1d was much more attractive – it was much less expensive and delivered passengers directly into the centre of town.

At the height of the First World War, passenger numbers began to fall, and locomotives were urgently needed for war service. Consequently the NER suspended the service from March 1917 with the intention of reopening the line at the end of hostilities. This however was not to be the case until 1920, but soon the doubts about profitability returned and fares were yet further increased. The line continued to operate but returned an annual loss of £3,000.

The loss of customers due to increased fares and the growth of motor bus services by road was to be the death knell of the Brampton branch line. The final blow however, came with the reorganisation of the national railway system in 1923. The NER became absorbed into a larger organisation – The London and North Eastern Railway (LNER).

Soon after the reorganisation was completed, the LNER terminated the lease of the Dandy branch line with Lord Carlisle.

All traffic to Brampton Town station ceased in 1923, the coal staiths closed and the "Dandy" track was lifted in 1924. The metal girder bridge spanning the Alston road was left intact until 1942 when it was removed as part of the wartime campaign to turn scrap metal into battle tanks.

The Dandy line remained an abandoned ruin for many years but became a popular footpath and in the 1950s it became an official footpath for part of the way. The Rowbank section through Rowbank Woods fell into private ownership with the woods now sectioned off with different names:

12. OH NO, NOT AGAIN?

Brampton Parish Council took over the ownership of the remainder of the line as a public footpath which is greatly used, but…

Brampton town, still does not have a convenient railway station.

By the Same Author

LIFE IN BRAMPTON WITH 63 PUBLIC HOUSES

David Moorat's gazetter of the surviving pubs of Brampton is a grand read. But more than that, it shines a light into dark corners of forgotten history; into the dusty attics where the really interesting snippets of past lives linger. If like me, you tend to remember pubs as navigation aids you'd better set aside a couple of days for the journey next time you venture Brampton way.

History Into Print, 978-1-85858-313-6, £12.95